The Story
Of Storm Cat

The Race Horse

MICHAEL PRICE

Copyright © 2009 Michael Price

All rights reserved.

ISBN: 1-4392-5407-9
ISBN-13: 9781439254073

Visit www.booksurge.com to order additional copies.

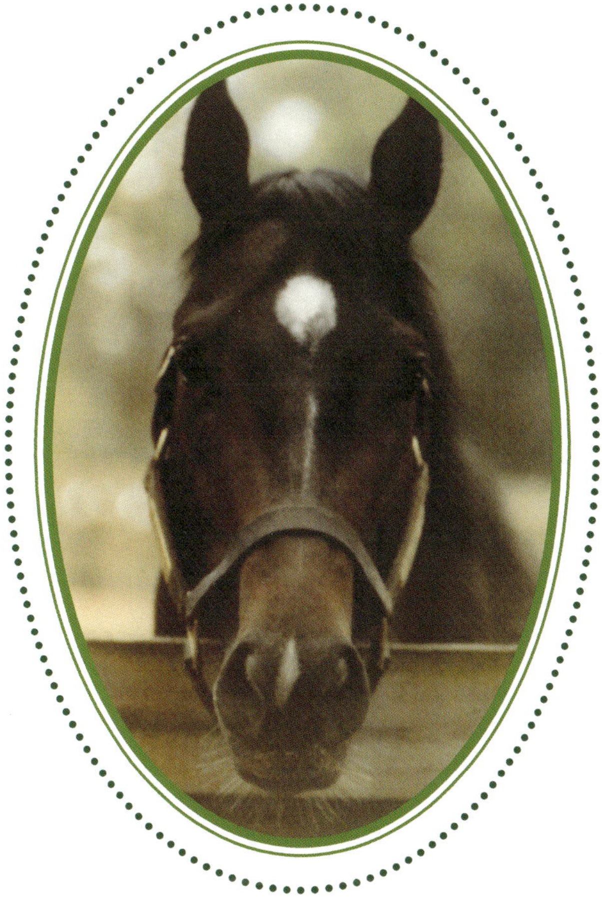

Preface

I hear so many times that Storm Cat was a very mean and hard to handle horse. I don't know where these stories came from but they are far from the truth. Well, now it's time that you learn the truth because as a race horse there was absolutely nothing what so ever mean about Storm Cat and I'm going to give you the truth and tell you his story as a race horse because I'm the one who was there with him, his race track groom, Michael Price.

Storm Cat was a high-spirited feel good kinda horse, who required a tuff fearless person to care for him and to keep him in check. And I think that is the same for most of his off spring. You have to take control right away before they do. That usually takes someone that is tuff and not afraid. (An animal reflects the handler's personality) You have to get to know the animal's personality and feelings. Developing trust and respect are very important with Storm Cat's off springs. (This is true with all animals.) Storm Cat was an extremely smart horse and I assume that he has passed that on. He also had the biggest heart of any horse that I have ever worked with; he never cheated, even in pain. He always gave one hundred twenty percent efforts. He had a champion's heart. I believe that all of our set backs are the reason for Storm Cat not being the two year old champion of the year.

I am very blessed to have had Storm Cat in my life and to be able to share our story with you. I hope that my story will help understand his off spring a little more and with it takes to handle them and to read the story of Storm Cat as a racehorse. Everyone knows Storm Cat as a famous Stallion but not as a racehorse. Well, now it's time to know, first handed.

Thank you and God Bless!

Michael Price

The Story of Storm Cat The Race Horse

My name is Michael Price. I am from a small town in Ohio. Bridgeport is on the Ohio River, across the bridge from Wheeling, West Virginia. As a kid (fourteen years old) I was introduced to thoroughbred horse racing by my cousins, W. J. Marshall and Freddy Jackson, who were trainers at Wheeling Downs in 1959, I started hot walking in the morning before school and then on weekends for fifty cents a head. Then in the summers, the horses would go to the meet at Waterford Park and I would spend my summers at Waterford.

I started grooming for a man named P. F. Fisher, an awesome boss. Back then, those old timers really knew their stuff. I learned how to make my own mud, to do horses up, to use your hard and soft brushes, and to have them when you brush your horse and finish with your burlap rub rag. And you had to learn how to pop your rug rag.

My cousin and all the other old timers taught me a lot and that is when the seed was planted. It all came natural to me. I have never had any fear of horses, just love and respect. The old timers taught me how to have pride in my work. They took a liking to me and they all joked with me. It was now deep into my blood. I worked with horses until I graduated from high school in nineteen sixty-four.

I joined the Air Force in nineteen sixty-five. When I got out of the military, I went to work in factories, mills and spent eight years as an underground coal miner. I even worked as an Ironworker for several years.

In nineteen seventy-nine, during a two week vacation from the coal-mine, I went to Ocala, Florida to visit some friends. It was like WOW!!! I saw beautiful farms and beautiful horses. It just blew me away. Being that I already had horses in my blood, Ocala rekindled my desire to be with racehorses again.

When my vacation was over and I went back to work, I couldn't focus on being a coal miner or anything else anymore. I just wanted to get back into the horse business. So three weeks later I gave up my job and all of the UMW Benefits, free medical care, etc. and one hundred dollars a day!

I packed up what I needed, took my two Dobermans, and moved to Ocala, Florida. My first job was for the Murty Brothers Farm. I made one hundred twenty five dollars for a six days week. It was very depressing, at first, to go from one hundred dollars a day to one hundred twenty-five dollars a week, but I knew that I was good with horses, so I decided to bite the bullet, hang in there, and learn.

At Murty Farm, I was around horses like Slew O Gold, Slewpy, Megates, and Only Queens. We had a few of Seattle Slews off-springs and I got to meet the owner of Slew. They sent their two-year old to trainer Jr. Serna. I learned a lot from Jr. and others at the farm. Barry K. Swartz also had horses there (Only Queens was mine) BK had sent a man to monitor his horse's progress and to check their conformation. I would ask him what he was looking for and he showed and taught me a lot about conformation. The more I learned, the more I wanted to learn. This was so awesome. Being in Florida working with offspring's of famous horses and meeting famous people. The "in your blood" thing was really flowing. I had not one regret for leaving the coal-mine, my family and friends, even my girlfriend. You have to make sacrifices to make gains. To me, it was all worth it because I was living a dream, just following my journey. (Life is death without adventure and adventure comes to those who are willing and daring enough to take chances.)

I learned a lot at the Murty Farm. Now it was time to move on and to learn more elsewhere and learn the other part of the business. I went to work at Happy Valley where I learned more but wasn't happy in that Valley, so I moved on. Then I went to other farms. I wasn't feeling anything at these places and wasn't happy. It was less like working somewhere just to get enough money to eat and pay rent – trials and tribulations.

Then one day it hit me. Colts and Stallions have always been my favorites (Fury and The Black Stallion). So I went to a Stud Farm, Hillview Stallion Station. I put in an application and got the job. It was like WOW again! I was in awe, these big, bad, beautiful stallions, Norcliffe, Barachios, Diamond Prospect, and El Rastro. My boss was an awesome man by the name of Hubert Pilcher. I consider him my friend. He was strait up with me and taught me how to handle and to take care of the Stallions. He was my teacher. He is the one who taught me.

To see the big, beautiful stallions transform, when it was breeding time, just amazed me. Hubert gave me my chance to work the breeding shed it was awesome. I did well because I had the best teacher. Hubert handled the studs and me the mares. I learned to twitch hold the left front leg while the stallion mounts its mare so that she won't kick him (boots on mare) as he dismounts. I spin the mare away from the stallion so that she doesn't kick him. Sometimes the mare would want to kick because she felt violated. I got to met and handle a lot of very nice successful and well-bred mares and meet a lot of wealthy and well-known people.

I was happy again. Then someone recognized my talent and ability and offered me a job as stallion manager at a farm called Heather Hills. Listening, learning, asking a lot of questions, being polite and respectful, and the love for what I do was really paying off. I only had three stallions and it wasn't breeding season yet. The stallions were Graustark Lad, Native Aid, and a full brother to Conquistador Cielo, Cielo's Dam. KD's Princess was there at the farm. I was in charge of the operation but it was boring because there was no action and everything became routine. The farm had a lot of broodmares and babies. It was sale time so they asked me to help and get some of these yearlings ready for the sale at OBS, I wasn't happy about it, because I was a stallion and colt man, not mares, or yearlings.

Some older man at the sales barn across from us came up to me one day and introduced himself t me and said that I was a super good groom and said he saw how I transformed that long haired baby to a beautiful dappled horse in a week's time. Amazing he said. Then he said that you could tell a good groom because you never know that they are in the stall. Never hear a lot of loud roar, stand up here, etc. Your horses are relaxed. Then he told me that he was a pin hooker and was the mayor of Stark, FL and we became friends. I forget his name, but truly remember him. He taught me how Pin hooking worked and what it was about. Once again, it was learning time.

Then he introduced me to a trainer from Savannah, GA. The lady and her boyfriend offered me a job on the racetrack in Atlantic City, NJ. But after the sale (OBS) they were going back to GA for a while but when they were ready to go to Atlantic City they would call me.

A couple months went by and I hadn't heard from them so once again I was getting bored with my job. I met this very classy woman named France Weiner while I was working at Hillview Stallion Station. She would send some of her mares to our studs. Well, I heard that she was looking for a new farm manager, so I went and talked with her and she gave me the job. IT was like WOW!!!, once again! Everyone wants a farm manager job and I got it. It was like the hit mother lode. I was so happy, a place to on the farm to live, a nice salary etc. WOW!!! All the living arrangements had been made etc. In the meantime, my mother calls me and tells me I was to get in touch with a lady from Savannah, GA. I call and they said that they needed me ASAP to go to Atlantic City. So now it was like, now what do I do. The farm manager job would be hard to turndown. But also, it was time to graduate from farm life and get back to the track where it all started. I needed to be back where the races were. After all, these are racehorses. So I thought and prayed about my decision and chose the track.

One of the hardest decisions that I have ever made in the business was to tell Miss France Weiner that I had to turn down the job. I felt very bad then about telling her the disappointing news and even to this day, I still feel bad about it. I am very sorry Mrs. Weiner and hope you understand that I had to follow my journey and my dreams. I am truly sorry.

Well, I ended up at Atlantic City Race Course, nice place – 1982(?). I was excited to be back on the racetrack – first time since 1964 that was my senior year in high school. Now it was time to put to use what I learned in Florida and to learn much more. After a while with this, I didn't seem to be learning much more than I already knew. So I went to another trainer who was a good horse person and a good teacher.

She taught me more. Another man gave me a job with more money. I took it and he taught me much more. He was difficult to work for so once again, I had to move on. Was working for someone else when one day a black man named Otis stopped me and said "Hey, I have been watching you and you have a lot of talent and as long as you are in the those stalls, no one will ever recognize it, and I can help you. I can help you become a horse dentist, a blacksmith, or a Jockey Valet." Right away, I said that I would like to become a Valet. I thought to myself, WOW!!! That's where all the action is, and I would love to be part of it. Otis said OK and to meet him at the track kitchen tomorrow at noon. I was there and so was he. He told me to go to the jocks room at 6 p.m. and ask for Joe Skinner.

I went there and introduced myself. He liked my interview and hired me right then. He introduced me to the man who would be training me - Billy Wilson (Mister). He was the master. He took me under his wing and taught me to be one of the best there is when it comes to handling those tough and unruly horses. Number one, he taught me safety. So now, I was a licensed Jockey Valet. WOW!!! I was just blown away each and every day by just going to work as a Valet. Here I was working with the best horses, the best jockeys, and the best trainers in the country. There I met a trainer named Johnathan Shepherd. It seemed like Shepherd would win all of the Grass Races. I liked Johnathan.

When Atlantic City closed for the season, Delaware Park was reopening and Joe Skinner asked me to come to work for him as a Valet at Delaware Park. I had proven myself as a quality Valet (I was taught by the best) - my friend Billy (Mister) Wilson.

I went to work at Delaware. I needed a groom job so I went to work for Ross Pierce, Buckland Farm Stable, good horses, good pay, but a hell of a lot of work and hours. I didn't like it, so I knew Johnathan Shepherd was there. Something about him and his horses interested me and someone told me he needed a groom. I talked to the Shepherd's foreman, he hired me, and I left excited about my new job. He gave me four horses to rub and there was no pressure. On my first day on the job, Johnathan didn't get there until a couple hours after we started. He had horses at different locations to attend to. He seemed a little surprised to see me there. He knew who I was because I had talked to him before in the paddock in Atlantic City. He seemed pleased that I was there working for him. He knew that I was good with horses. Plus I was the oldest and most experienced groom that he had, so he gave me pretty good horses to rub and I felt good about where I was.

All he had to do was tell me what to do to my horses and it was done and with pride. I took my time with my horses, never in a hurry to get done and gone. I got to know Jonathan's girlfriend and now wife (Kathryn Montgomery) pretty good and she and I always talked about the horses. Kathy cared about the horses and she knew that I did also. We became pretty close. Johnathan never talked about much. He seemed quiet and shy. But he wasn't.

It was always nice to see him smile or laugh. But he and Kathy didn't have a lot of time to hang around.

After all of the sets were done, because he had horses at other tracks to tend to. I worked for Johnathan until the end of the season in December. Then I went home to Ohio for the Christmas Holidays then to Tampa Bay Downs for the winter.

Someone had told the Jocks Room custodian in Tampa (who was looking for a Valet) that I was a Valet up in Atlantic City and Delaware Park and that I was good at it. So one day while I was grooming on the backside they paged me to come to the jocks room. I didn't know what was going on. I went to find out what it was about and the boss told me that he heard I was a Valet and asked me to work for him. So for the rest of the winter and that meet I was once again working on a groom and a Valet and loving every bit of it. It gave me a very nice feeling.

I had really come a long way since leaving the coal-mines and starting over in Ocala. Hard work and being determined to be good and successful to have the love for what I was doing was paying off and I was really blessed and happy! Then after the meet at Tampa was over it was time to get back up to Delaware to get back to work for Jonathon and the Jocks Room as a Valet. Everyone was glad to see me and I was glad to see them and to be back in Delaware.

When I got to the barn, Vito said to me "Mike I got two new horses that I want you to take and one of them is supposedly a pretty nice two year old named Storm Cat. He said to check them out. When I looked in Storm Cats stall, he was munching on some hay and not paying attention to anything. So I asked Vito what was so special about him because he didn't seem to be real big or outstanding and Vito said because he was Royalty Bred. He said that his mother, Terlingua, was a champion by Secretariat and his dad Storm Bird was a champion by Northern Dancer and I thought to myself WOW!!!!!, All famous champions and sires, Northern Dancer, Sire of Sires.

So I decided to go back down to Storm Cats stall to get a better look and feel for him. So I climbed under the webbing to go check him out. He was still eating his hay. I reached out to grab him by his halter, he turned around and tried to seriously bite me, and it wasn't for play. So that is how Storm Cat introduced himself to me. So I decided to introduce myself right back. I gave him a reality check and told him that he was going to learn to respect me and that I would respect him. I liked him already because I could see that he was a fiery dude and I liked his attitude. He wasn't afraid of anything. I was excited because I thought WOW! This is my kind of horse. When I look him in the eye, it was like looking at a human eye because they were so smart. He had that smart protruding eye. It was like he would move his eyes and look at you like a human would. He was always checking me out trying to find away to do something to me. Then I realized that I couldn't let him outsmart me. I had to be on my toes and stay one-step ahead of him. He was extremely smart.

Before I got Storm Cat, whoever handled him before me didn't take control. He did and could get away with whatever he more or less wanted to. They didn't know how to handle him, he handled them. But when I came along things had to change. He started to trust and to respect me, but he was still always full of himself and ornery and always looking for an opening to get you. It was like a game to him. But I allowed him to play his game as long as he didn't get out of hand and I wouldn't allow that to happen and he knew that so he began to respect me more because he knew that if he didn't then he had a price to pay, (Michael Price). It was so neat, because when I walked him I had to always keep my eye on his eye because if I would look away, he would get me and when he did, you could almost see it in his eyes that he was smiling and saying uh huh, I got you. But it was cool, because he was just a smart ornery kid, who was having fun and I allowed him to be that. It made him happy and kept him tuff. It was an awesome bonding that we were having

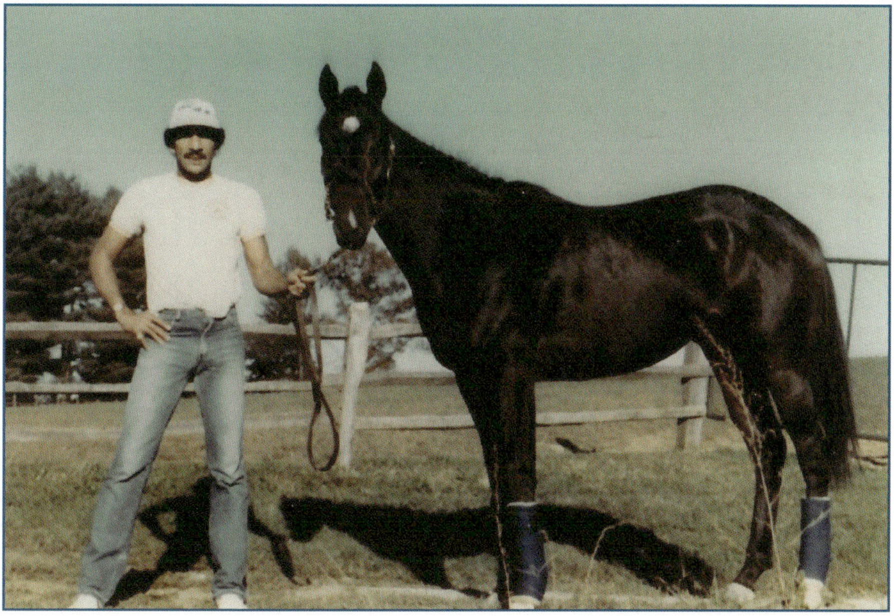

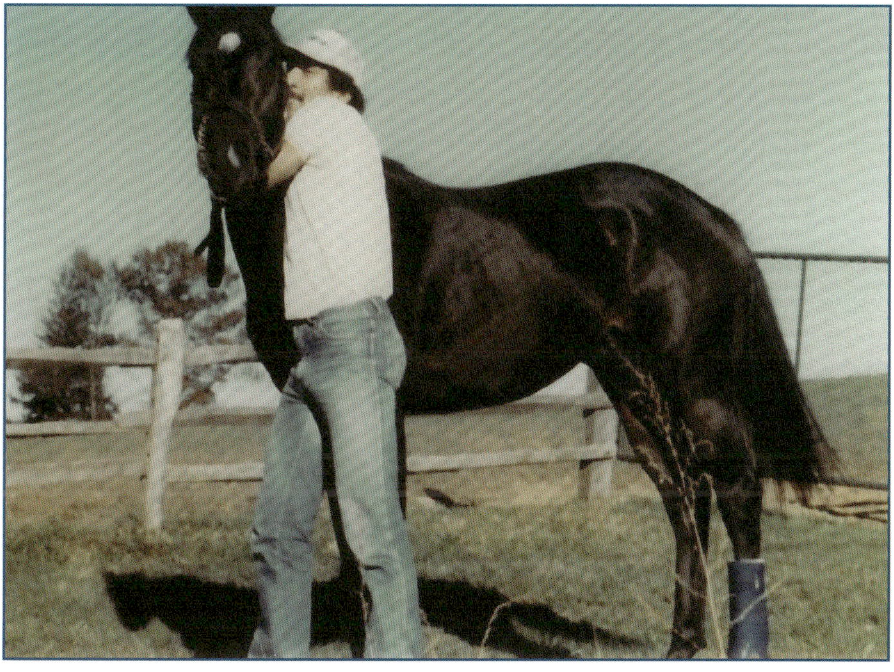

I had never been around a horse that was as tuff and smart as he was. The ones who had worked with him were somewhat afraid of him. No one wanted to walk him because he was a bear to walk, always full of his self. Just a feel good guy, who liked to buck, prance, and dance around the shed row. I was his groom and his hot walker. I didn't want anyone else to handle him because I had him how I wanted him and I just couldn't and didn't trust anyone else with him except for a couple of people on Jonathan's Farm.

There was not a mean streak at all in Storm Cat, just a competitive streak. His main thing was trying to bite you and that was it. He never used his front or back feet to try to hurt you. When I walked him, he would always buck and kick but never at anyone. He just loved to play, but without control, his play could get out of control and he knew how far he could go with me. He was so smart he was making my life with him fun and exciting. He was different from any other horse that I been around and knew that he was something special. It was almost like working with a human.

Storm Cat and me had made such a bond that one day I called Johnathan to the side and said to him that I had never before ever wanted to spend my career with any one horse but Storm Cat is different and I want to always be with him even after he retires from racing. Johnathan said he doesn't normally do that but for Storm Cat and me he would make an exception and allow it. It was like WOW!!!, together, forever, during his racing career – Papa and me. I never called him Storm Cat, Cat, Storm or anything other than PAPA, (that's all I ever called him). But I also wanted to be with him when he retired from racing and went to the breeding

He was bringing the best out in me and I was doing my best to bring the best out in him. Johnathan was allowing me the freedom to do what I felt needed to be done unless he would have other plans.

It was so neat, two tuff beings and athletes, me and Papa (Butch & Sundance). I always had him looking good. He always looked like a million dollars, beautiful deep dappled and shiny beautiful mane, and tale. I never used a regular comb on him. Only brushes one hard, one soft, rubber curry-comb, and nice burlap rug-rags. His bandages always looked like they were sprayed on. Not only was he a smart bad ass, he was also very proud and very handsome. I was very proud of him and to be with him.

The training continued at our no need to hurry pace. Storm Cat was really eager to do his thing. He was a bear but it was cool. Then it came time for his first big work out, the five-eight mile. I was very excited. It was time to see him do his thing and the whole barn was excited. Kathy was on him and is a known jockey. So, he had a real jockey on him and not an exercise rider. I walked Kathy & Storm Cat up to the track. Got my binoculars (which I had never done before), jumped in the car with Johnathan and rode over to the grand stand to watch from there while Johnathan timed him with his stopwatch. He was working in the company of two other horses. He was on the inside (rail) when they got to the half mile pole and the horse next to him pulled up to him and stuck a head in front of him and thru my binoculars I could see it in his eye that when that horse went ahead of him that really ticked him off. So he just gritted his teeth, pinned his ears back and dug in and the rest was history. I could see in Jonathan's face that he was moved and so was I. What I saw thru those binoculars just blew my mind. I truly saw that competitive fire in him. I saw it in his eyes and that was for real. I will never forget that. I know that what we were all doing was working (The conditioning, the feeding, & the caring). It made me want to do even better than I had been doing to help make him even better.

It was August of nineteen eighty-five and Saratoga was open and Johnathan had just previously won the leading trainer title and he was also steeplechase king. Especially with his Champion Eclipse Award winning steeplechase horse, Flatterer. So Johnathan was spending a lot of time at Saratoga because he had a barn full of horses up there. Storm Cat and I were still in Delaware. Well it finally came time for Storm Cat to go for his first race, a maiden special, he came in second. Johnathan decide to keep him there for a second maiden special and he won. This was good news but sad for me because I was still a Valet at Delaware Park. I wasn't able to get time off to go with my horse. So, for the first time, we were split up and I had a hard time dealing with it because I knew that no one could give him what he was used to. No one really, really knew him but me. I was very concerned about how he was going to finish. Well race day came and later on, I got the news that he had won. I was very, very happy but sad because I wasn't with my horse. Not long after his race, he was sent back to me at Delaware and it was great to have him back. I said that I would never be without him again.

He came back to me, sound, so I was pleased with that. So, now, I was back doing my thing with him to prepare for our next race, which would be the World Appeal at the Meadowlands with Magambo and Danzig Connection, who were well known at that time. The jockey, who rode Storm Cat on his maiden win, got the call again. Storm Cat took the lead and started to pull away but Danzig Connection was on the outside and Storm Cat started to get out and the jockey started whipping Storm Cat left handed which kept making him get out even more and he didn't correct it in time and we interfered badly with Danzig Connection and his jockey claimed a foul, (We won). We were disqualified and placed second. There was no excuse other than a very bad ride. That was a bummer, but my horse did his thing and we beat quality horses and he came back sound.

I realized that when it was race time and he got his game face on, you had better be ready because he really became a handful to handle but I had the situation under control. People really had to get out of his way. He would know that it was show time and he would really get fired up (in the paddock).

Then it was time to get him ready for his next race, all was going well and no problems. I had always spent a lot of time with Storm Cat, but now I was spending more time with him because I wanted to do my part to help him get even better because he was good. When training was done and all of the horses were groomed and fed, the other grooms and hot walkers could not wait to get out of there but not me. I didn't care what time it was, I just cared about my horse and he was my friend. He enjoyed me being around as much as I enjoyed being around him.

He loved when I groomed him. He was a little ticklish and really like to nip at me when I was rubbing him then when it was to do him up (bandages) I gave him his head and he would go for his hay. He was so cool, so smart, and very comfortable with me and trusted me to as when I was putting on his bandages I always crawled underneath him to get other side to do the other legs and he would never flinch, just kept eating his hay. After I was finished and took his halter off, I would just stand outside of his stall and just admire him and the job that I had just done on him. He always looked handsome, shinny and healthy, it was being proud of him and pride in my work. It would give me a rewarding feeling.

On one occasion Johnathan came in and gave me some exciting news, we were going to run in the five hundred thousand dollar Graded Young American Stakes in the Meadowlands. Once again, WOW!!! Five hundred thousand dollars, this is for real. We were all excited, but Kathy and I were super happy because we knew what we had in our horse. We knew that he would win. Storm Cat had a three-furlong work for preparation with Kathy on him. His work was awesome; it was a black type work, best work of the day anywhere. WOW! I saw it in the racing form the next day.

We were ready. The entries came out and I was even more confident because we were going to be running against Magambo, Danzig Connection, etc. Then there was Groovy who was best known for his speed. I didn't think that his speed would hold up that far, a mile and one-sixteenth, and I wasn't worried about the others because we had beaten them before. I told Johnathan that we needed a new rider after the World Appeal because the last jockey didn't fit our horse and he made the change. He signed Criss McCarron to ride Storm Cat. I was happy about the change. Now I had even more confidence in winning and my horse was sharp as a tack, anxious to rock and roll.

Okay, it's race day. The race was to be televised on ESPN, so I called my friends and family to watch the race. Now they would be able to get a picture of why I had so much love for what I was doing.

Post time – once again he was a bear in the paddock because he knew that it was show time. He broke well, Criss put him in a nice spot, took his time and at the three-eighth pole Storm Cat made his move, but it was trouble because he couldn't break free but then he got that look in his eye that I had seen before, gritted his teeth, pinned his ears back and dug in to win by maybe a neck. That race really showed me the kind of heart that he had. He could have given up and gotten beat, but he was determined not to let that happen. I thought to myself what an athlete, what a competitor and that's the way I've always been myself, so I was somewhat emotional, because I could see me in my horse and him in me and that's one of the main reasons why my relationship with Storm Cat was so special. We had a lot in common I have always been an athlete and a very serious health and fitness person. Always training myself, I was able to apply my knowledge, fitness, and health to my horse. I always felt like his personal trainer and massage therapist. I have had enough injuries and soreness in my days to know how to treat them, so that made working on Storm Cat even more fun, exciting and mostly preventative. I think that is one of the reasons Johnathan gave me the freedom to care for Storm Cat and do as I felt was needed. I had never been that freedom with any other trainer. He let me do my thing. My job was to do everything that I could to bring the out the best in Storm Cat and in return, he was bringing out the best in me. I can do the best that I can to put my feelings about my life with Storm Cat into words but there are feelings I can't describe.

The Young American Race took a little out of Storm Cat. It was a hard fought race and he was a little tired and had some minor soreness. But I went to work on it all and in no time, he was back to his ornery self. Training and everything was going well. Storm Cat was full of his self as usual and really wanted to run.

Then I also grazed him a lot. He really enjoyed that. When I would first take him out to graze he would buck and kick but then settle down to eat. But I had to really keep a close eye on him because at anytime he might try one of his tricks.

More time had passed and one morning Johnathan, once again, came with great news, we were going to the Breeders Cup. The Breeder Cup Juvenile, WOW!!! This was about as good as it gets for a two year old. It would be in front of the whole world, on national TV, at Aqueduct with all of the best horses, trainers, and owners. I felt so blessed and fortunate to have this opportunity with the horse that I had. Once again, I thought to myself, I'm a long way from the coal mines. I called everyone that I knew to give them the news.

I had my horse looking good and he was as sharp as he could be. He knew that it was getting close to that time.

It was race day, a cloudy, overcast, and chilly day. I was in awe. Here we were, The Breeders Cup. The best of the best and we had one of the best. Storm Cat was getting his game face on and he knew it was race time. We drew the outside post position and were in with some of the same horses that we have beaten in the past.

Storm Cat broke good, he was on top and McCarron got him to relax and he settled in and at the three eight pole he made his move, took the lead again, and started to draw away. We were in front and home free, then about fifty yards from the wire; a horse was flying on the outside and closing very fast. It was <u>Tasso</u>, a supplemental entry from the west coast that I had never heard of. He was up with Storm Cat at the wire; it was very, very close.

I ran down to the track and Johnathan was right behind me. I turned around and he looked at me and said "Mike I think he got beat". I said don't say that, because I think he got it. It was so close that it seemed like it was taking forever for the results. The results came and we got beat. It was as close as it could be without being a dead heat, losing a race that close really hurt. It would have been easier to handle if we were beaten by a length or more. That hurt, it really hurt!

That race took a bit out of him. He was sore. We got him back home and Dr. Copelan came and checked Storm Cat out. X-rayed his knee and found that there were bone chips in that area. He had run the race with them and he didn't let them slow him down. That's the kind of heart and courage that he had that of a champion. He was my champion. Well, our season was over.

The decision was made to have the bone chips removed from Storm Cat's knee. So that meant that we would have to be separated for a while. He was scheduled to have the surgery done at Ohio State University by Dr. Bill Copelan. After it was complete, he would be sent back to the farm (Overbrook) for his recovery.

In the meantime, Johnathan and most of the help went to Camden, SC for the winter. I stayed in Philly to work as a non-union iron worker until it was time for me to get Storm Cat back. I just kept working to kill time until I got my call from Johnathan. When that day came, I got the call from Jonathan's secretary on the farm saying that Storm Cat was in Camden, SC and that I was needed there ASAP. So the next day I left my iron working job, stopped by the farm office in PA as instructed to get my travel expense and instructions and get back with my horse. I was also told that Storm Cat needed me right away. I was so happy that there is no way for me to put it in words. There was a big void in my life without Storm Cat. He was my partner.

My girlfriend and I set out set out for Camden. It was so beautiful when we got there... We went straight to the training center. The help was glad to see me and I was glad to see them. But they were really glad to see me because they wouldn't have to deal with Storm Cat any more. They were all very afraid of him. They said they had to tranquilize (ACE) him each morning to walk him and all of the help would stay in the tack room until his walk was over.

I went to look in on my horse and what a surprise! He had really matured, put on a lot of weight, and filled out really nicely. He was a beautiful, better looking animal. I walked into his stall and he gave me the same greeting that he gave me when we first met. He seems as if he kinda forgot who I was, I grabbed him by his halter and said to him, "Hey Papa, it's me, what are you doing?" Then it seemed to hit him, he remembered me. He looked at me as if he were really happy to hear my voice and to see me again. But he seemed a little sluggish and right away, I knew that it was from the ACE. And I knew that it wasn't good to have him like that, so I told the foreman that I was here now and that my horse didn't need any more Ace. I was his tranquilizer.

So next morning when I came to work it was time, once again, Storm Cat and me. He wasn't doing any training yet, just walking. Remember we were bringing him back after having surgery and being out of training. He had grown and matured so much and so eager to get to work that he was tougher than he had ever been and one of the reasons was that he had people so intimidated that he was once again getting away with things. So when I started walking him, without the Ace, he started doing his thing but I had to give him a reality check and then just like that he came to his senses. It was like it all came back to him and it was like old times. I was in my world. Some of the people there didn't know who I was, they had never seen me before and I heard someone say, "Who is that guy walking Storm Cat?" and someone replied "That's Storm Cat's Michael". They were amazed to see how cool he was with me. I had my horse back and we were doing our thing once again (Butch and Sundance).

Johnathan and Mr. Young really managed this horse very well and put together an awesome comeback program, taking our time. They had this huge round pen built for Storm Cat; it looked like a giant wooden barrel. It had a lot of very deep sand in it and a little platform to stand and view him inside.

The first day that we took him there and turned him loose, we were really curious to see how he was going to take to it. The purpose of the pen and the deep sand was to let him get some restricted room to run free and natural and to help build his legs up and stretch out the tendons. We wanted to let him get his exercise and let some steam off. We weren't ready to start putting tack on him yet. It was too soon after the surgery to start galloping. Everything went well. Storm Cat took to his new playpen very well. Then I began to lunge him in the round pen each day. It was so neat to see those newly matured muscles of his (three years old) start to develop their tone again. I could see that the lunging was working. His legs, shoulder, chest, and rear end were really starting to look good. He was having fun being back at work again.

Then came time to tack him up, at first it was just around the shed row, then came the time for him to go to the track. Everyone at the barn was excited because most of them hadn't seen him in a long time under tack. I was really excited because this meant that Storm Cat's three year old season was now beginning. All went well that trip. It was nice and easy. He really enjoyed it. Training had increased and Storm Cat was doing well.

Johnathan moved Storm Cat and me to the other side of the training center where we were by ourselves. It was so neat, privacy all to ourselves, quiet, pretty and surrounded by tall Pines. Storm Cat and I had our own private little world back there that made him so much more relaxed because there were no distractions back there. He had his own paddock that I turned him out into every day and he had plenty of nice green grass that I would graze him on every day. He was in heaven back there and so was I.

The track and the turf at the training center were both very hard because there hadn't been any rain for a long time. So Johnathan decided not to train Storm Cat on that track because it was too hard for our horse and not what we needed at this time. So there was this trail behind our barn that went thru the pines. It was a deep sandy trail and it led to a very deep sandy track maybe a half mile oval and that's where we started galloping him. It was so amazing how Storm Cat was developing into this powerfully built and handsome three-year-old race horse with a different attitude. He seemed more serious and professional about his work. He made me so proud to be with him.

Now it came time for Storm Cat to start galloping in company. He couldn't have asked for better company, it was Flatterer, a Johnathan Sheppard trained champion. Johnathan always galloped Flatterer and Kathy would be on Storm Cat. Every time those two horses trained together, it just blew my mind. To me I was looking at two champions and I used to think to myself, it's too bad that I'm the only one seeing this, a once in a lifetime sight.

Johnathan and Kathy would fly back up north to tend the horses at the farm in PA and the other horses that were racing. So when Kathy wasn't there her sister Maria would get on Storm Cat. It was always such a nice beautiful trip thru the woods to that training track and Storm Cat was always so relaxed, but when he hit that track a powerful machine, and a real handful for Maria. I would always hear her calling "Kitty", that's what she called him.

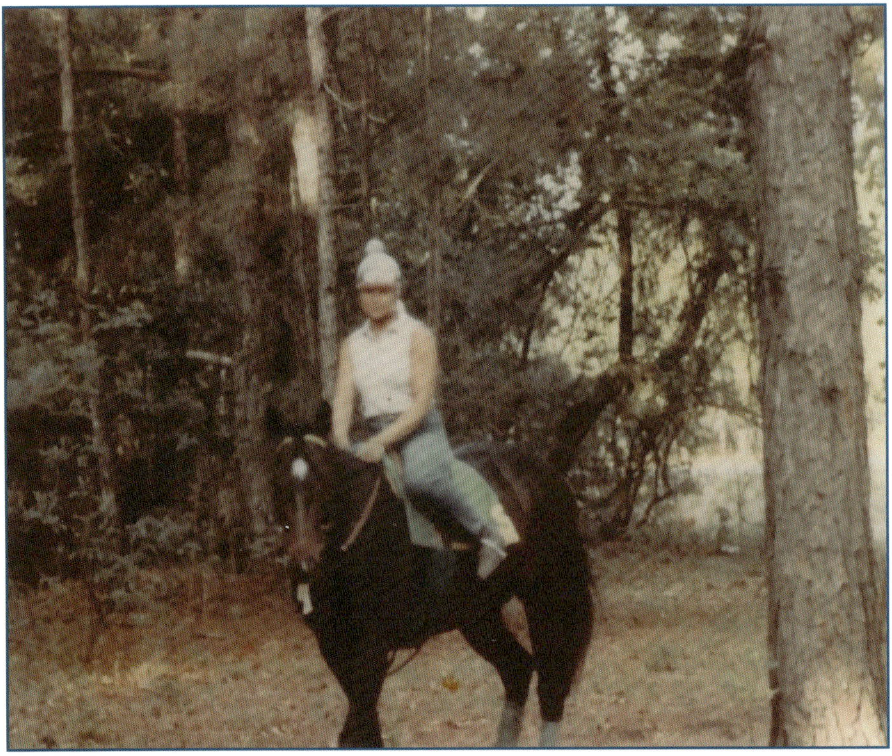

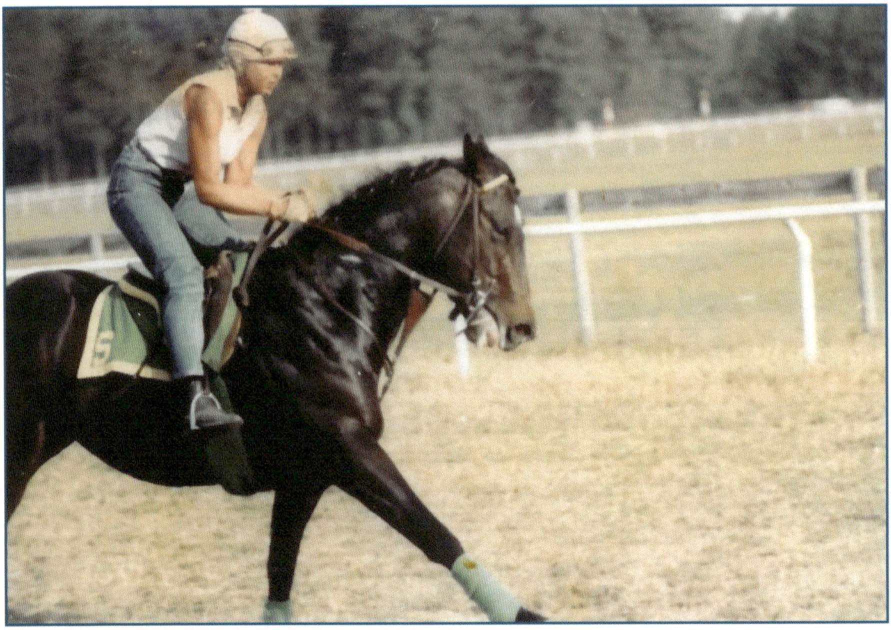

She was trying to get him to settle down. (Maybe he didn't like her calling him Kitty because he was to macho to be called Kitty)

I think our goal was to get Storm Cat ready for the Met Mile, which was a ways off but we were too. So there was no hurry. Johnathan and Mr. Young wanted to do things right and I wasn't in any hurry either.

As time went on, Johnathan felt that it was time to put Storm Cat back on the main track (turf) and start him galloping there. Johnathan had him and Flatterer galloping in company more often.

Everything was going great, and then one morning, Marie took Storm Cat for his gallop. He was really on the muscle and went a little bit strong but not bad. So when Marie pulled him up and started jogging back to me, I could see that Storm Cat was off in his right front. I got the worst feeling because right then I knew that we had a problem. The closer they got to me, the more apparent it became. I said, Marie we have a problem and she said I know. She dismounted. I started felling his legs and low and behold, he had just popped a splint on the inside of the cannon bone near the suspensory ligament, I knew that I needed to go to work on it right away. He was halfway cooled off by the time we walked back to the barn. I gave him a quick bath. I was going to hose the leg down with cold water, but it was so hot there that the cold water was warm. So my sports medicine mind kicked in, I went and got some ice from the Fridge in the tact room, crushed it up and placed it where the popped splint was and used Saran Wrap to keep it in place and then a bandage over that. Called the shed row boss and told him to come over right away. He got there and I told him what had happened, so he called the vet, who got there pretty quick. Told him what happened, he removed the bandage and ice, felt the leg and asked me to walk him. Then he determined what the problem was and he told me that the quick action that I took with the ice was the best thing that could have been done. He told me that I really stopped the problem from being much worse than it could have been. I just did what I would have done if it had been me who popped a splint. Johnathan and Mr. Young were contacted right away. So, in the mean time, I did a lot of hosing and poultice.

Dr. Copelan flew down to evaluate the situation, had x-rays taken and commended me on the goo job that I had been doing and told me to keep up the good work.

So now it was back to just walking Storm Cat. He wasn't happy about that because he was getting fit and he really enjoyed working.

We were faced with another setback, but I was used to taking our time with Storm Cat, so to me, time wasn't the factor, just getting my horse right was the focus regardless of how long it would take. Once again, as an athlete, I know that you don't rush injuries because if you do then you will have a bigger problem later on. And that's how Johnathan and Mr. Young felt also. It was so nice working for them because it seemed that we were all on the same page. These different setbacks just helped you develop patience which I had been use to.

Dr. Copelan made another trip down, this time with Mr. Young. Dr. Copelan told me that at first his first look at Storm Cat that he was concerned that it could be over for our horse because of the location of the injury. But after more recent x-ray sent up to him in Kentucky , he studied them and said he was so concerned because being that the splint was directly over the suspensory ligament that it would put pressure on it, but he could see where the ligament was wearing a grove into the splint which was allowing movement and not restricting it. So he felt that if that continued to happen then we should be okay.

We finally got the ok to get back to work. I was still walking for now but after his walks, I started turning him out into his paddock so he then started getting his legs back and let off some steam. After he would finish all of his rolling around in the sand and his bucking and kicking (playtime) he would seem to get bored and then he would walk the paddock that is what we wanted him to do, once again in the deep sand. (I felt that the very hard surface on the track is what caused the splint problem.)

We then got the ok to get him tacked up again, walks and easy gallops, all was going well. His training began to increase and that was much to Storm Cat's liking, we continued his galloping and his condition was getting better.

Now it was time to leave Camden and head back to Delaware Park. Once we were back in Delaware, we continued his gallops and were back on a racing surface. Storm Cat was happy being back on the track and out there with other horses. He was still his everyday tough and full of himself kinda guy.

It was coming near the middle of July and the Saratoga meet was about to begin and Johnathan had a barn full of horses at Saratoga and spent most of his time there but still had to make his rounds to the far and the other tracks to check on those horses, etc. So he felt that it was best for Storm Cat to be in Saratoga where he could keep a close eye on him and his progress because he was increasing his training and getting ready to start getting him ready to race again. We only trained on the Oklahoma Track, which is a very nice track. It was so awesome being in Saratoga. What an experience, one that everyone in the business should be able to experience. Jonathan rented a nice big house for some of the other help and me right on Lake Saratoga and my being there with my big horse was a once in a lifetime experience, WOW!!!

Storm Cat made me feel special when we would walk to the track because when people realized who he was they all took notice and spoke to me. Many people would say "good morning, nice horse" and I would hear them talking about him and admiring him as we passed by. They remembered the Young American and Breeders Cup races and they knew that he was a force to reckon with. It was so neat because everyone started to know who we were, Storm Cat and me really blew a lot of people's minds because not only was I Storm Cats groom and hot walker but I was his Pony. Johnathan would ask me to jog (Pony) holding on to his chinstrap pacing him from the seven eight to the three quarter pole and breaking him off from there. Most people couldn't believe that I was doing it. At first, when Johnathan asked me to do it, I thought that he was joking but when I realized that he was serious, I said okay. So I was known as Storm Cat's Pony, kinda neat – Hot walker/Groom/Pony. But for us Saratoga was just a stepped up training period. The Saratoga meet was ending, so now it was time to load my horse into the van and head back to Delaware. It was sad leaving Saratoga because it was such a beautiful experience.

Okay, now we're back at home base. The splint problem is no longer a problem. His leg is fine and we got the okay to get ready to race. I had put so much focus on his leg that I was very

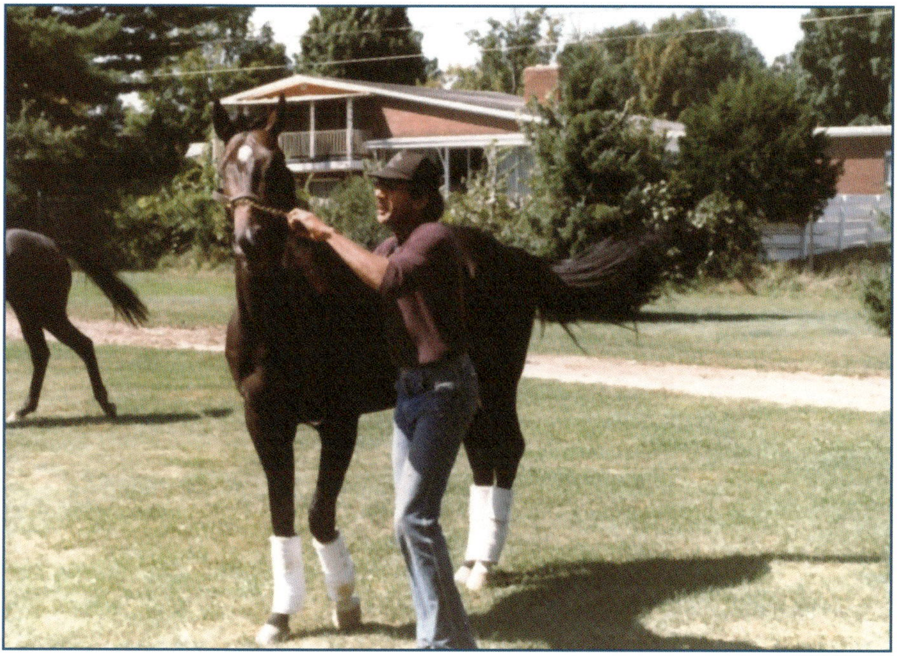

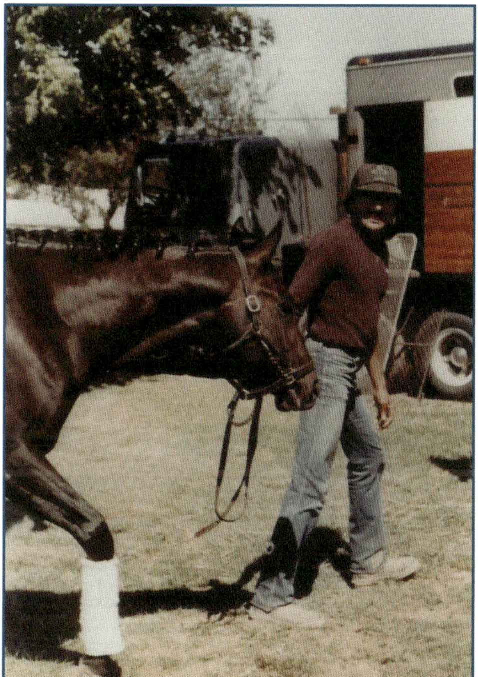

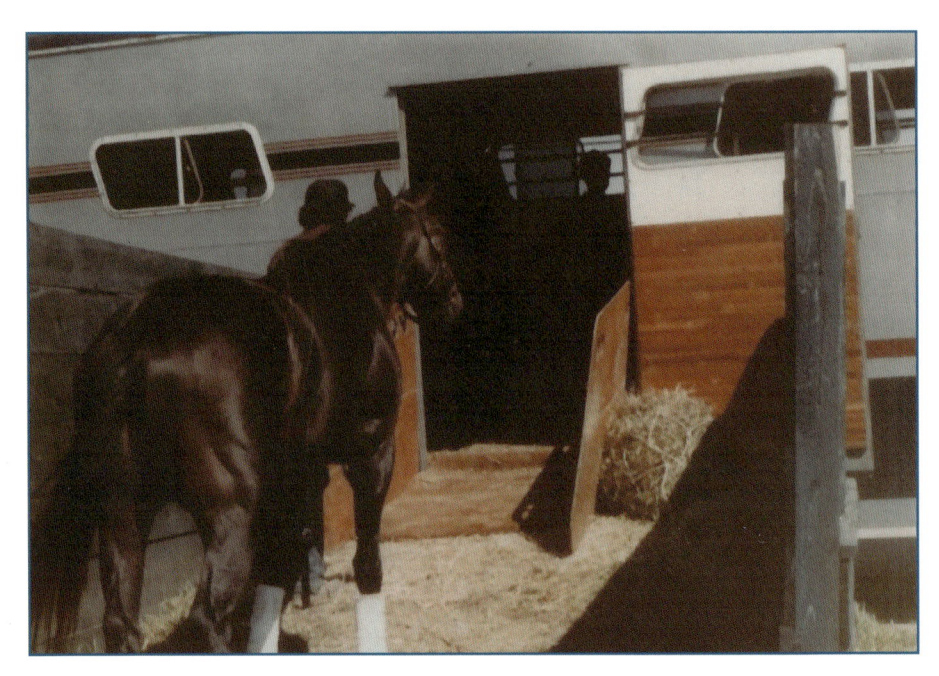

confident in it also. So now, we are really getting eager because now we knew that race day wasn't far down the road. Now it was time for Storm Cat to get a couple of good works under him, which he did, and they went very well. My horse was happy, healthy, and ready to run.

There was a race coming up in the Meadowlands, NJ for him, so Johnathan sent us to the Meadowlands to get him used to the track. Jose Santos came in one morning to work Storm Cat, his last work before his next race. Santos was impressed with how Storm Cat went. All is well; my horse is sound and ready.

Johnathan told me that my horse was entered in an allowance race on Halloween Night, oh was I excited. I finally get to see my big horse make his three-year-old debut; it had been a long time coming. We had really been thru a lot to finally get there.

Well, when race day got there and he wasn't fed he knew what was happening. Now it was time to get him ready for his race. They would soon be calling us to the paddock. Johnathan came over to the barn to make sure we had everything together and he helped me with the bandages. He was looking so magnificent, shiny, muscular, dappled, main braded and bandages looking good. We were ready.

They called us to the paddock. I put on his bridle, picked his fee, polished him off with my rub rags, and started on our way to the paddock. I said to Storm Cat, okay Papa, its show time, let's go do our thing. This is what we've all been waiting for his first race since the Breeders Cup.

Storm Cat was being calm on the way to the paddock. A sort of long and dark walk but then all of a sudden, when the bugle blew for the race that was going on the track, he changed right then. He knew what that meant and then he put his game face on and became that handful again. But I had him; I had to get a little bit heavy on the shank a few times to get his attention. Then we got to the paddock and then it was really on. He was tougher in the paddock, more than he had ever been. He pretty much cleared the paddock. Bucking and a lot of kicking, man, he wanted to run. He really made my job tuff that night, but I enjoyed it because it was kinda fun. It felt so good being out there with him because I knew that everyone was watching us. He was heavily favored to win. This time Rick Migliore rode him. Storm Cat warmed up very good. I was very nervous but confident that we would win. Okay now there at the gate, my heart is almost pounding out of my chest.

They break evenly, Storm Cat stayed near the lead and then at the three/8th pole he made his move. He went to the lead but it wasn't really easy to break clear, but he stayed in front and we won. How sweet it was, all of the hard work from the setbacks that we had all of the time this took to get here, all of the patience had paid off for all of us. What a beautiful felling. There were supporters from the farm who passed up a Halloween Party to be there.

Storm Cat came back good. It didn't seem like the race took much out of him. I took him back to the barn, gave him his bath, cooled him out, did him up, and fed him. Everyone came to see and congratulate him (Johnathan, Kathy, Marie and the guys from the farm. Dr. Copelan, Jim Cannon, and Mr. & Mrs. Young didn't make it to this race).

Storm Cat and I stayed at the Meadowlands for a couple more days before heading back to Delaware. I couldn't wait to get out of there. Been there too long and I didn't like it there.

We got back to Delaware and started getting ready for our next race. Everything was going good.

Then it came time for our next race, we had two choices, a race in New York or a race at Laurel, MD. The decision was made the morning of the race that we were going to MD. So we had to hurry and get ready because I think it was a two hour or more ride in the van. So we got loaded up and it was just Storm Cat and Me in the van on our way to MD. I started noticing something about my horse, I wasn't feeling right about how he seemed to be feeling, something wasn't right.

It was race day and he didn't seem to be in the mood to race. He seemed lazy like that fire and desire to race wasn't there today.

I had never seen him this way before. I did not feel good about the way he was going to perform today. I was really baffled because he was sound and all of that but something just wasn't right and I know my horse like a book.

When we got to Laurel and got off the van, I walked him around the shed row a few times and then put him in his stall. Johnathan came to the barn to make sure that we were okay, that all was well, and that we were ready. He helped me and put Storm Cat's run downs on, then he told me that he would see us in the paddock and then left. I put the finishing touch on my horse, and then they called for us to come to the paddock. On the way to the paddock my horse was walking along just fine when all of a sudden he heard the horses from the face before ours running and he came to life but not like before. He wasn't really tough to handle. A once we were in the paddock I was prepared for the usual. He was tough but not that tuff. Once the horses were on the track, he seemed to warm up okay but he didn't even look the same out there. He looked sort of like and average horse, he didn't seem to stand out.

The horses reached the gate and I'm getting nervous about this. They all break good. Storm Cat was near the lead but when it was time for him to make his move, it wasn't happening, it still wasn't happening and it never did happen, he finished a bad fourth and was beaten by horses that weren't even in his class.

Something was really wrong and I knew from the beginning in the van that something wasn't right. He came back sound after the race. Legs, knees, ankles, and tendons were all just fine. He didn't seem to run hard enough to cause any problems. We were all confused and very concerned as to what the problem was. So we took Storm Cat back to Jonathan's Farm. They had the vet come in and run some test and to take some blood.

Well once again another setback. Training was stopped until we got the results from the vet. Well, finally, we got the results and once again, the news wasn't good. Storm Cat's White blood cell count was down. So once again, my horse was taken out of training. It was now December getting close to Christmas and Storm Cat was idle and I was lost without my horse. It was cold and I was bored. It was time for everyone to get ready to go south for the winter and me to go spend the holidays with my family in Ohio. There wasn't much I could do with Storm Cat right now and I knew that we would be apart again until he got better and it was time for me to go home. So I spent some farewell time with my horse, to let him know how much he meant to me and how much that he had changed my life and that I was never his exercise rider or his jockey but he had taken me on one hell of a ride. Then I gave him a big hug around the neck and said to him "Thanks for everything and I'll see you later Papa!" That was a very, very emotional time for me. It was really hard to leave him that day and I honestly think I saw a tear fall from his eye. I wasn't really sure that he would ever race again. We had been thru a lot, one set back after another. I sort of felt that enough is enough and we gave it our best shot.

Then it became official, there was another problem that occurred, and Storm Cat was retired from racing. When Storm Cat retired from racing, I officially retired from grooming. I have never groomed another horse since I did everything that I could on my part to help bring the best out of Storm Cat and in return, he brought the best of in me. I feel that nothing could ever compare and what I gave to Storm Cat I could never give that to another horse. So I feel that it wouldn't be fair to me to another horse or to anther owner or trainer for me to not give them my very best, because I couldn't because I had already given my very best to the very best, my friend Storm Cat. I hadn't forgotten that I would like to be with Storm Cat after he retired. Well, I meant that.

So I got in touch with Mr. Young and told him how much I wanted to stay with my horse. He pretty much said okay but he arranged a meeting with farm manager Jim Cannon and me.

So I drove to Kentucky to Overbrook Farm and once again WOW!! Jim met me and gave me a grand tour of the whole farm. I got to see Terlingua, Storm Cat's mother, and many more famous horses. Jim took me over the whole farm. The stallion barn wasn't even built yet, but Jim showed me where stallion barn & breeding shed were going to be built, etc. It was almost like he was giving me the red carpet treatment. I was very impressed with all that Jim had showed me. He offered me the job, a place to live and more, but most of all a chance to be with my horse once again and forever. WOW!!! A dream comes true.

In the mean time, Mr. Young was at the Keeneland Sales and I wanted to go there and hang out and hoped that I would be able to spend some time with Mr. Young. I found him and when he had a break he and his secretary and I went to some room, got a table and talked about Storm Cat, the job, etc. That was another big moment being with Mr. W. T. Young at the Keeneland Sales while he was spending big bucks on horses. It was a very nice visit and experience. I told them that I would let them know what my decision would be after I got back home, I thought about everything, over and over, and I knew from my experience of working, in breeding business in Ocala, that during breeding season you were busy. It got to be too repetitious for me and then when breeding season was over, then it was all farm work and I knew that I would eventually get bored.

While I was still thinking about what to do, I got a call from a friend who wanted me to come to work for him as a jockey valet at a new track in Birmingham, AL. I had given up my job as a valet at Delaware Park to be with Storm Cat, I missed the excitement of being a valet and all of the fun in the jock's room, and we were all like one big happy family. We don't have to work a lot of hours and we have two days a week off. My friend told me that the job was mine if I wanted it. I told that I would get back to him and let him know. Would it be Storm Cat or would it be being a valet again? So I chose to go back to being a full time valet and that's what I'm still doing today.

I let Mr. Young and Jim Cannon know what my decision was and they understood. It was a hard choice but I had to do what I felt was best for me... I thanked them for all that they had done for me and the opportunity to be part of a very, very special horse and I promised to always stay in touch and that I would periodically come and visit my horse

I have kept that promise. I periodically call and check on my horse and I go to visit him on occasions. When I go visit him they allow me all the time that I want with him. I usually hang out with him for a few hours whenever I visit. It's so neat, because he always remembers me. He's usually out in his paddock and all I have to do is say "Come here Papa" and he takes his good ole time and moseys over to me and, as always, the first thing he does is try to bite me. Once again, I have to keep my eye on his eye. I just hang out with him and reminisce on how it used to be, and then I usually take pictures of him.

Being that Overbrook allows me the freedom to come and visit Storm Cat whenever I want, makes my decision to go back to being a valet much easier because I still can have Storm Cat in my life.

Dedication and Thanks

Dedicated in memory of Mr. W. T. Young, without him the Storm Cat Era would have never been. He revolutionized thoroughbred horseracing. Thank you, Mr. Young, for the gift that you gave me, Storm Cat.

Special thanks to Jonathan Sheppard for believing in me and trusting me to care for such a valuable and special horse and giving me the freedom to do the things that I did for Storm Cat. Jonathan you're the best!! Thank you.

Kathy, special thanks to you also for believing in me and always complementing for the job that I did on our horse, also for looking out for me and Storm Cat. You and I always knew how special Storm Cat was and we always shared our thoughts and feelings about him. THANK YOU!

A very very special thanks to my awesome cousin Oliver **(Sonny)** Newsom for all the help in putting this project together because without him I really don't know what I would have done. Sonny was like my seeing eye dog during this project. I love you very much and thank you.

I dedicate this in memory of my mother, Amanda. Mother knew who Storm Cat was and what he meant to me. My Mom was my best friend in life, my biggest supporter, and fan. My Mom was a very spiritual lady. Before she passed on, she gave the best compliment that I could ever have received, she said to me "Honey you are very blessed!".

Well my experience with Storm Cat was one of those blessings. There are three things that are on my mind every day of my life, God, My Mother, and Storm Cat. WOW!!!

Thank you Papa!!!